A+ books™

Shapes around Town

Triangles
around Town

by Nathan Olson

Capstone press®

Mankato, Minnesota

A+ Books are published by Capstone Press,
151 Good Counsel Drive, P.O. Box 669, Mankato, Minnesota 56002.
www.capstonepress.com

1 2 3 4 5 6 11 10 09 08 07 06

Library of Congress Cataloging-in-Publication Data
Olson, Nathan.
    Triangles around town / by Nathan Olson.
        p. cm.—(A+ books. Shapes around town)
    Summary: "Simple text, photographs, and illustrations help readers identify triangles found
in a city"—Provided by publisher.
    Includes bibliographical references and index.
    ISBN-13: 978-0-7368-6373-5 (hardcover)
    ISBN-10: 0-7368-6373-7 (hardcover)
    1. Triangle—Juvenile literature. I. Title. II. Series.
QA482.O476 2007
516'.154—dc22   2006005633

Credits

Jenny Marks, editor; Kia Adams, designer; Renée Doyle, illustrator; Kelly Garvin,
    photo researcher/photo editor

Photo Credits

Capstone Press/Kay Olson, 24–25
Corbis/Alan Schein Photography, 18; Andrea Jemolo, 6; Richard Cummins, 21; Richard Klune, 9;
    Roger Ressmeyer, 7; Yang Liu, 13; zefa/H. Spichtinger, 23; zefa/K. Hackenberg, 20
Getty Images Inc./Photodisc Blue, cover; Photographer's Choice/Adam Crowley, 16
Image Farm, 26–27
Richard Cummins, 10, 12, 22
Shutterstock/Melissa Dockstader, 8
Superstock/age fotostock, 14–15, 17; James Lemass, 4–5; Richard Cummins, 11, 19

Note to Parents, Teachers, and Librarians

The Shapes around Town set uses color photographs and a nonfiction format to introduce readers to
the shapes around them. *Triangles around Town* is designed to be read aloud to a pre-reader, or to be
read independently by an early reader. Images and activities help early readers and listeners perceive
and recognize shapes. The book encourages further learning by including the following sections: Table
of Contents, Find the Triangles, Welcome to Triangle Town, Glossary, Read More, Internet Sites, and
Index. Early readers may need assistance using these features.

Table of Contents

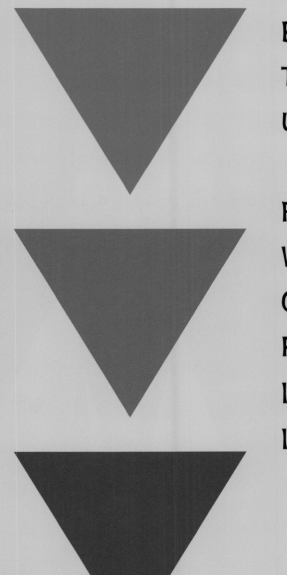

What Is a Triangle?

Triangles are flat shapes with
three sides and three corners.
Let's look for triangles
all around town.

Every triangle has three
sides and three corners.

Two triangles can form a diamond shape. Diamonds have four sides and four pointy corners.

Building Triangles

Builders pound and hammer to make triangle shapes for houses. How many triangles do you see?

A house called an A-frame looks
like one giant triangle.

Triangles top the homes on this street. Do you see small triangles inside the larger ones?

These shiny triangles are made of glass. Rooftop windows let the sun shine in.

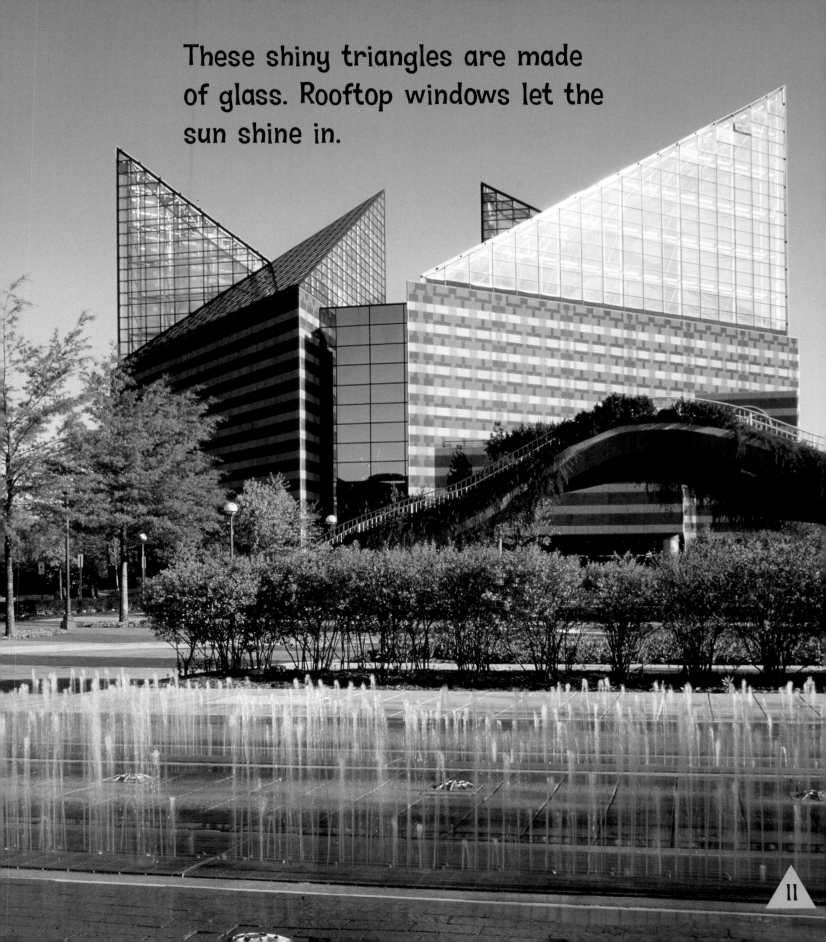

Big stone triangles greet visitors
to this business.

Look up! Tall triangles are stacked up to the sky. Triangles support buildings and make them sturdier.

Triangles in arches keep a bridge strong. Cars and trucks can travel safely across wide rivers.

15

This bridge's grate has hundreds of tiny triangles. Rain and snow fall through the grate so the bridge won't get too slippery.

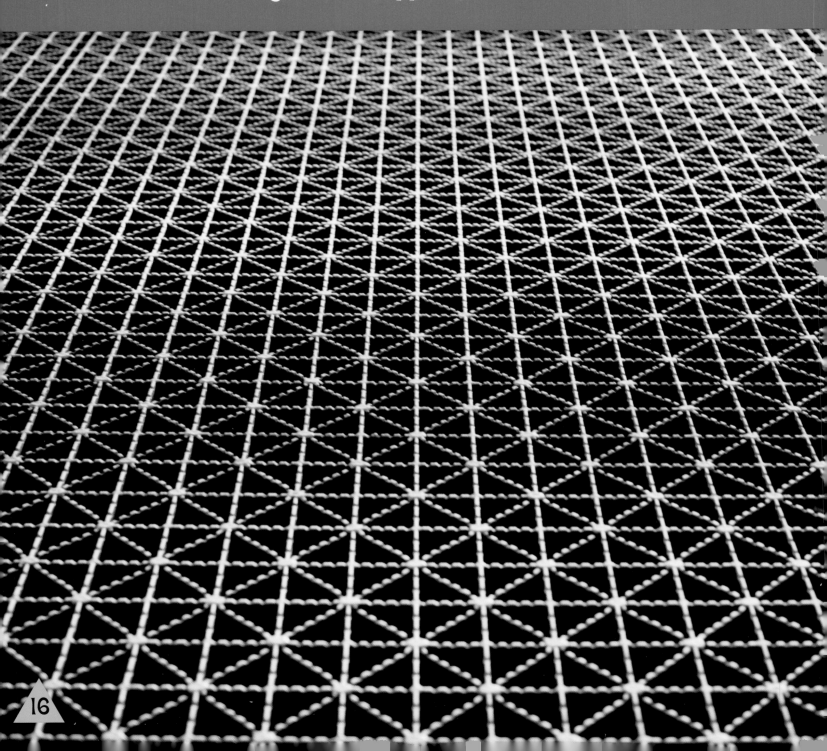

Triangle braces made of steel
hold train tracks high above
the water.

Unexpected Triangles

This ride at the fair spins you high in the air. Look closely and you'll find triangles.

The giant jack-o'-lantern at the market has triangles for its eyes and nose.

Triangles sometimes hide inside letters or numbers. Where is the blue triangle?

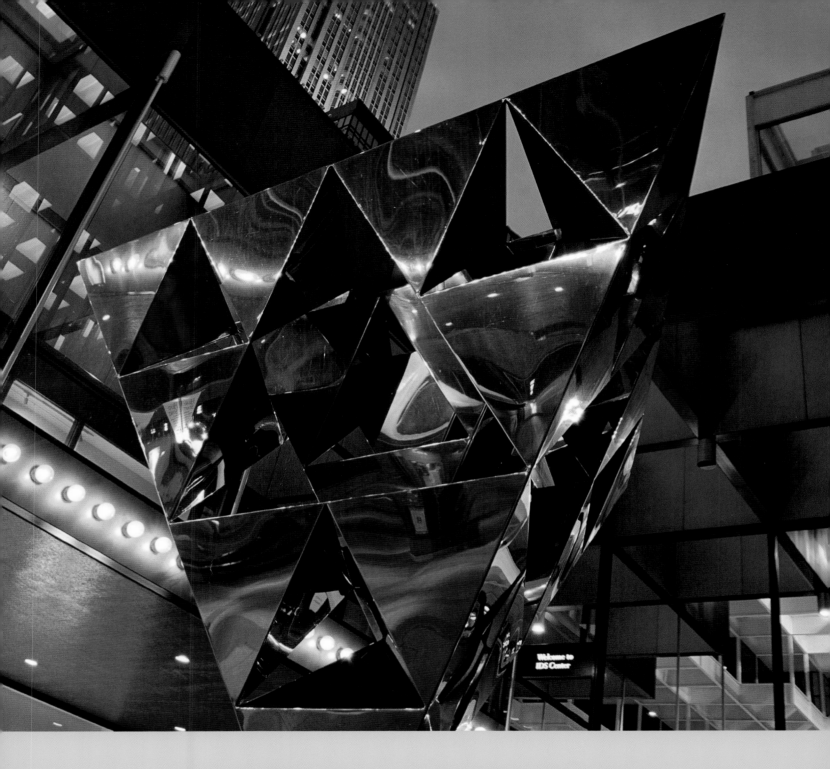

Shiny glass triangles reflect lights,
buildings, and streets. Even the spaces
between the triangles look like triangles.

The playground has lots of fun
triangles you can climb
or play inside.

This famous statue is crowned
with triangles. It's called the
Statue of Liberty.

Triangles appear in so many places. How many can you find in your town?

Find the Triangles

Triangles are flat shapes with three sides and three corners. Which of these signs are triangles?

Triangle Town is full
of triangles of all sizes.
Where do you see triangles?

29

Glossary

arch (ARCH)—a curved structure that helps support buildings and bridges

diamond (DYE-muhnd)—a shape with four sides, like a square standing on one of its corners

grate (GRAYT)—a grid of metal bars that lets snow and water pass through; cars drive over grates when they cross bridges.

jack-o'-lantern (JAK-uh-lan-turn)—a pumpkin with a painted or carved face

reflect (ri-FLEKT)—to show an image of something on a shiny surface such as a mirror

support (suh-PORT)—to hold something up or keep it from falling

Read More

Campbell, Kathy Kuhtz. *Let's Draw a Fish with Triangles.* Let's Draw with Shapes. New York: Rosen/PowerStart Press, 2004.

Jones, Christianne C. *Party of Three: A Book about Triangles.* Know Your Shapes. Minneapolis: Picture Window Books, 2006.

Leake, Diyan. *Triangles.* Finding Shapes. Chicago: Raintree, 2006.

Internet Sites

FactHound offers a safe, fun way to find Internet sites related to this book. All of the sites on FactHound have been researched by our staff.

Here's how:

1. Go to *www.facthound.com*
2. Select your grade level.
3. Type in this book ID **0736863737** for age-appropriate sites. You may also browse subjects by clicking on the letters, or by clicking on pictures and words.
4. Click on the **Fetch It** button.

FactHound will fetch the best sites for you!

Index